Cryptocurrency

Effective Strategies For Profitable Crypto Day Trading
And Initiation Of Investments In Bitcoin And
Leading Altcoins For Substantial Gains With Minimal
Risk

Damon Howe

TABLE OF CONTENT

Purchase Bitcoin Globally From Any Location

A myriad of methods exist for the acquisition of Bitcoin in nearly all nations, encompassing avenues such as gift cards, bitcoin ATMs, local traders, brokers, and exchanges. This provides an in-depth exploration of the process of procuring Bitcoin irrespective of geographical location.

You may be familiar with Bitcoin, the unconventional form of digital currency. You might now be inclined to further explore the revered pinnacle of financial technology, the harbinger of the future in the realm of finance, the transformative force in payment methods, the digital equivalent of precious metal, and the solution to eliminating barriers in capital restrictions. The most effective approach to acquiring knowledge is through personal experience. Acquire a unit of

Bitcoin, utilize it to execute a transaction, store it within your digital wallet, and observe its value oscillate. Nevertheless, from where do you acquire it? And how is it accomplished?

Acquiring one's initial Bitcoin can be an intimidating endeavor for numerous individuals. It would appear to be an exceedingly formidable task. Nevertheless, this is not the situation. There are a plethora of choices available for expeditiously, conveniently, and effortlessly acquiring your initial Bitcoin transaction.

The determination of the best option is contingent upon your specific geographical location and individual preferences.

TLDR:

1. Acquire Bitcoin using conventional fiat currency. 2. Obtain Bitcoin through the exchange of traditional fiat currency. 3. Procure Bitcoin by converting

standard fiat currency. 4. Secure Bitcoin by purchasing it with conventional fiat currency.

2. Provided you possess a wallet, it is viable to acquire Bitcoins on a Bitcoin exchange by means of a conventional payment method, such as a credit card, bank transfer (ACH), debit card, interact, or E-transfer.

Subsequently, the Bitcoins are transferred to your cryptocurrency wallet.

Nonetheless, prior to determining the most optimal method to acquire your initial Bitcoin, it is imperative to contemplate the ensuing variables:

•To what extent are you prepared to disclose personal information?

• What is your preferred method of payment? • In what manner would you prefer to make payment? • May I inquire about your choice of payment method? • Kindly indicate how you would like to settle your payment.

- May I inquire about your place of residence?

You should possess the capability to systematically ascertain the platform that most suitably aligns with your requirements, taking into account these aforementioned factors.

This manual commences by delineating the options for divulging personal information (or abstaining from its disclosure) and the available modes of payment accessible to you. The guide delves into the most prevalent methods of purchasing Bitcoin, along with a comprehensive overview of multiple exchanges spanning across different nations.

PROCEDURES FOR ACQUIRING BITCOIN GLOBALLY

Private Information

Bitcoin is regarded as a financial instrument and, consequently, it is subject to regulation in most jurisdictions. Nearly all websites offering Bitcoin transactions or facilitating buying and selling of Bitcoins are subject to the widespread implementation of Anti-Money Laundering (AML) regulations. In order to authenticate the identity of their customers, the majority of these platforms are required to adhere to the regulations set forth by Know Your Customer (KYC) laws.

Due to the fact that Bitcoin transactions are stored openly on the blockchain and can be traced, the level of personal information disclosed during the process of purchasing Bitcoins carries notable privacy consequences.

There exist numerous stages of KYC, with each necessitating the disclosure of progressively more personal information. Below is a comprehensive enumeration of the grades, commencing with the least favorable:

• Lack of Know Your Customer (KYC): In the absence of a KYC, the identity of the user remains undisclosed to either the network or the Bitcoin seller. It is not necessary to exhibit identification or make payment using cash, Moneygram, Paysafecard, or Western Union. In certain legal jurisdictions, the acquisition of Bitcoin without adhering to Know Your Customer (KYC) requirements is permissible. This can be accomplished through means such as Peer-to-Peer (P2P) marketplaces like LocalBitcoins, Automated Teller Machines (ATMs), or Gift Cards. However, it is important to note that this approach generally incurs higher costs compared to alternative methods.

• KYC Enhanced: This tier of Know Your Customer verification utilizes your provided payment channel and/or registered contact numbers to authenticate your identity. Payment providers possess knowledge of your identity regardless of whether you make payments through your bank account,

PayPal, credit card, or another commonly used payment method. By employing KYC Light, individuals have the capability to purchase a restricted quantity of Bitcoins across numerous platforms, encompassing direct exchanges, trading platforms, and online marketplaces.

•Complete Customer Due Diligence: In addition to utilizing your phone number and bank account for identity verification, Complete Customer Due Diligence necessitates the submission of supporting documentation to establish your identity. A passport, an identification card, a driver's license, a utility bill, or a combination thereof may be employed. Certain platforms may necessitate the involvement of a notary or a reputable intermediary, such as your financial institution, in order to validate your identification documents. Alternatively, some platforms accept the submission of a photograph depicting yourself alongside your identification card, or may request your participation in a video verification procedure. If one desires to engage in substantial monetary transactions or participate in trading activities on exchanges, it is generally unavoidable to undergo Full KYC procedures.

What would be the most optimal approach to acquire Bitcoin?

Bitcoin functions as a form of currency; however, its acquisition requires the transfer of funds to a designated recipient. The greater the sophistication and efficacy of your nation's financial system, the less arduous it becomes to exchange your currency for Bitcoins.

The primary obstacle that deters Bitcoin trading is the circulation of antiquated fiat currency. If you opt for a payment method characterized by slowness and high expenses, the acquisition of your Bitcoin will be gradual and come with elevated costs. One can expedite the purchase of Bitcoins by utilizing a swift medium.

Below is an incomplete, non-comprehensive compilation of prevalent methods utilized for purchasing Bitcoin:

• Electronic funds transfer: The electronic transfer of funds is well-known to the majority of individuals. Usually, funds are transferred to a Bitcoin vendor and, upon the completion of payment through online banking, Bitcoins are received. The typical duration in the majority of countries falls within the range of 1 to 3 days. Direct debit is not widely acknowledged. The vast majority of exchange platforms solely accept bank transfers as the exclusive mode of payment.

• Payment Method: Credit cards are extensively utilized across various transactions. Nevertheless, only a limited number of primary merchants accept credit cards. The rationale behind this is that Bitcoin transactions lack the capacity for reversibility, while credit card transactions possess this feature. The merchants who have been accepting credit card payments have incurred losses due to this situation. Suppliers frequently encounter the possibility of individuals acquiring Bitcoin through the use of stolen credit cards. Exploit the potential of illicitly obtained credit card data through Bitcoin transactions, employing sophisticated algorithms to mitigate associated risks.

• PayPal: While there are a few websites that do accept PayPal, the majority of them are opposed to its use, citing similar concerns associated with credit card transactions, namely the ease with which PayPal transactions can be reversed. The vendor may incur a loss if this event transpires subsequent to the buyer transferring the acquired Bitcoin to an alternative wallet. This elucidates the rationale behind the inadvisability of engaging in Bitcoin trading on the eBay platform. Nevertheless, there are certain websites, such as those that deal with credit card transactions, that are willing to accommodate payments via PayPal.

• Alternative Payment Methods: (Sofort, iDeal, Skrill, etc.): There is a plethora of payment service providers available in the realm of commerce. There is a considerable number of them within the European Union, solely within its borders. A considerable quantity of direct exchanges bolsters an array of options. If you opt for a widely-used provider like Sofort in Germany or iDeal in the Netherlands, it is highly probable that your domestic direct exchange will be compatible with it.

• Alternative payment channels such as cash, Western Union, and Paysafecard are generally not accepted by the majority of commercial platforms. There is a limited number of trading platforms, and it is highly unlikely that any direct exchanges will accept these forms of payment. In p2p marketplaces, it is common to come across sellers who are willing to accept cash or alternative non-public payment methods. A viable alternative would be to consider utilizing an automated teller machine (ATM) that facilitates the purchase of Bitcoin using physical currency.

What is the most economically efficient approach to acquiring Bitcoin?

We are making significant progress towards the acquisition of your Bitcoin. In this particular segment of our comprehensive guide, we will present to you a selection of esteemed models for the conversion of traditional fiat currency into digital cash, specifically in the form of Bitcoin. Every individual model possesses its own array of advantages and disadvantages.

• Bitcoin Automated Teller Machine: A Bitcoin automated teller machine represents, arguably, the most straightforward and confidential means to acquire Bitcoins. Those automated teller machines that facilitate cash withdrawals using personal identification documents such as passports, I presume you have encountered them before. Certain companies, Lamassu being an example, produce Bitcoin automated teller machines that facilitate the acquisition of Bitcoin through cash transactions. The operators of these devices have the option to utilize a variety of Know Your Customer (KYC) regulations, which encompass methods that range from cellphone verification to the implementation of biometric techniques. A comprehensive map displaying the locations of these devices worldwide can be found on Coin-ATM-Radar.com. An alternative form of automated teller machine (ATM) operates by utilizing an established ATM network for the purpose of vending Bitcoins, typically available in banking institutions or railway stations. This accomplishment has been realized in countries such as Switzerland, Ukraine, and Spain. A considerable proportion of automated teller machines impose a fee ranging from 3 to 6 percent, and in some cases, even higher.

•Electronic Vouchers: An alternate method for acquiring Bitcoins is through the use of electronic gift cards or vouchers. One would need to visit a kiosk or alternative retailer in order to acquire a gift card or voucher, subsequently proceeding to access a designated website and input the code designated on the card in order to acquire Bitcoin. This methodology is employed in Austria, Mexico, and South Korea, along with numerous other jurisdictions. Gift cards, similar to automated teller machines (ATMs), have gained notoriety for imposing excessive fees.

• Direct retailers: These merchants resemble the currency exchange facilities typically encountered at airports, but with enhanced interactive capabilities. They employ a digital marketplace to acquire Bitcoins, which are subsequently dispensed to their clientele in exchange for currency. To obtain Bitcoins at the fixed rates offered by the platform, one must navigate to a website, select a preferred payment method, make the payment, and subsequently receive the acquired digital currency. The majority of these platforms necessitate the possession of a personal wallet, although certain alternatives such as Coinbase and Circle provide the convenience of utilizing their own offered wallets to store and transact with your Bitcoins. Given that these platforms facilitate a diverse array of payment options, encompassing credit cards and PayPal, they present themselves as the swiftest and most expedient avenue for novices to procure their inaugural assets in the form of Bitcoin. The charges associated with direct commercial exchanges vary between 1% and 5%. All individuals stand to gain from the disparity in purchase and sale rates. The majority impose supplementary charges for the utilization of such payment methods, including credit cards.

• Peer-to-Peer Marketplaces: Individuals engaging in the buying and selling of Bitcoin convene and conduct transactions on peer-to-peer marketplaces. The charges applied on these markets are relatively minimal, varying between 0 to 1%; the extent of the difference is primarily influenced by the liquidity of the market and the chosen payment channel. In contrast to a direct transaction, one has the opportunity to place a bid, wherein the prospective buyer determines a specific price and patiently awaits a seller to offer a Bitcoin. This enables one to acquire significant volumes of Bitcoin at comparably affordable prices. LocalBitcoins is widely recognized as the preeminent peer-to-peer marketplace. This international market accommodates multiple currencies and grants the freedom to buyers and sellers to select their preferred mode of payment. It is frequently employed to facilitate anonymous transactions, often at excessively high rates. Bitcoin.de, the largest peer-to-peer (P2P) marketplace in the Eurozone, boasts robust liquidity and serves as a convenient platform for the conversion of Euro currency into Bitcoin. Bitsquare is widely recognized as the third prominent peer-to-peer market, operating solely as a software entity that facilitates linkage between individuals in a fully decentralized manner.

•Exchange platforms: If you intend to purchase significant volumes of Bitcoin at competitive daily rates or engage in Bitcoin trading, it is likely that you will require the services of an exchange platform. Exchanges function as custodians for their clients, safeguarding both Bitcoin and fiat currency in escrow. You may submit your buying or selling orders within this platform, where the trading engine of the exchanges compiles these orders and brings together offers from both buyers and sellers to facilitate trade executions. On numerous occasions, exchanges provide a wider range of trading possibilities, including margin trading. Fees and spreads are typically negligible. Nevertheless, the process of establishing an account on an exchange can pose challenges as it entails divulging personal information and placing trust in the exchange to safeguard your financial assets.

Exchanges, wallets, and financial institutions have all been duly cautioned.

Irrespective of the verification requirements for establishing identity, it is important to bear in mind that the level of security provided by exchanges and wallets does not parallel that of financial institutions.

Take the following illustration into consideration - in the event that the exchange becomes insolvent or falls victim to a cyber attack, as exemplified by the highly publicized case of the ill-fated exchange Mt Gox, it is possible for your account to encounter either insufficient or limited safeguards.

In specific regions across the globe, Bitcoin lacks the status of being legally accepted as a means of payment, thus leading to authorities occasionally encountering difficulties in formulating appropriate strategies to address incidences of theft. Subsequent to a fraudulent incident within the exchange, larger financial platforms have duly restored customer funds; however, it is important to note that they are not presently bound by legal obligations to engage in such restitution.

Comparing Bitcoin And Ethereum: A Comparative Analysis For Determining Superiority

• Bitcoin is a distributed digital currency that operates on a decentralized network structure, enabling direct and secure transactions between users without the involvement of intermediaries. Transactions undergo verification by network hubs utilizing cryptographic methods and are securely stored within a decentralized public ledger known as a blockchain.

• Ethereum is also a decentralized digital currency, however, it surpasses being solely a payment system. Similarly, a platform enables designers to create and execute decentralized applications (dAps). These decentralized applications can be leveraged for creating a wide range of solutions, spanning from intelligent contractual agreements to the establishment of autonomous and self-governing Decentralized Independent Associations (DAOs).

Comparative Analysis: Evaluating the Superiority of Bitcoin and Ethereum

In the year 1999, esteemed Nobel laureate in economics, Milton Friedman, expressed his belief that the Internet would emerge as a potent catalyst in diminishing the role of government. He held a parallel perspective regarding the absence of reliable electronic currency, and as he had foreseen, the emergence of the cryptocurrency Bitcoin in 2009 validated his prediction.

What is Digital currency?
Digital currency operates in a manner quite similar to conventional forms of money such as the US dollar, Euro, British pound, Japanese yen, Indian rupee, and others. One notable disparity between cryptocurrencies and government-issued currencies lies in their centralization. Cryptocurrencies are decentralized in nature, meaning that they do not possess a central authority, such as a financial institution

or governmental entity, exerting control over them.

Nevertheless, specifically, cryptocurrencies make use of blockchain technology, which comprises a collection of records organized within a container referred to as a block. These transactions are publicly recorded and subject to systematic oversight.

What is Bitcoin?

The digital currency Bitcoin was introduced in 2009 by an individual or a collective known as Satoshi Nakamoto. It enables global transactions, allowing individuals to send and receive funds across international borders. As mentioned earlier, the payments are secured through the utilization of cryptography. The utmost paramount aspect of Bitcoin resides in its capacity to preserve the anonymity of individuals engaging in the transfer of monetary funds.

It is widely acknowledged that whenever a transaction is conducted through a financial institution, a certain amount of money or service fee is invariably involved. However, when considering Bitcoin, this fee is exceptionally minimal, rendering it a more enticing alternative in comparison to conventional electronic transactions.

10: The Art of Interpreting Graphical Representations

Engaging in cryptocurrency trading often leads individuals to discover their latent interest in this field. Regrettably, it is prevalent for individuals venturing into this practice to harbor the expectation of amassing immense wealth within a remarkably short span of time. Although it is possible for individuals to acquire the skills to exploit market cycles for financial gain, there is no guarantee that all participants in this endeavor will achieve their objective. As previously stated, trading operates on a set of regulations; however, given that these regulations are self-imposed, it is common for individuals to violate them.

Regardless, the initial principle that every trader must adhere to is "do not invest an amount greater than your threshold for potential loss."

Our initial task involves acquiring the skill of interpreting stock market charts, commonly referred to as "Japanese candlestick charts" in technical terminology. While it is true that a line graph can visually depict the price trend, the candlestick charts provide a wealth of additional information that surpasses what can be gathered from observing a line graph.

The rationale behind the nomenclature of these graphs is readily comprehensible, as the visual symbols (depicted in shades of red and green) bear a striking resemblance to traditional candle shapes. Every individual candle displayed on the chart represents the price movement within the specific time interval designated by the user. Due to this specific rationale, it is customary to encounter charts spanning various timeframes such as 1 hour, 4 hours, 1 day, 1 week, and the like, each represented by a single candlestick.

Now, let us envision the examination of a one-dimensional (1D) chart, where it is understood that each candle symbolically represents the events that transpired within the previous 24 hours. Hence, a red-colored candle indicates a decline in price over the course of 24 hours, whereas a green-colored candle signifies an increase in price.

The vertical dimension of the candle symbolizes the fluctuation in the unit price. Upon observing a red candle, which serves as an indicator of a decrease in price within a given time interval, one can deduce that the upper boundary represents the opening price while the lower boundary represents the closing price of the trading session. Conversely, for a green candle, the upper and lower boundaries would represent the opening and closing prices respectively.

In certain instances, uncolored candles can be observed, exhibiting a significant resemblance to crosses. This particular candlestick pattern signifies that the initial price and the final price were nearly identical; the boundaries of these crosses (either pointing upwards or downwards) visually depict the price fluctuations (highest and lowest) that took place throughout the trading session.

Bitcoin Participants

There exist two distinct groups of individuals who utilize the Bitcoin system, and these groups may not necessarily be entirely distinct from one another.

• Users of the Bitcoin system conduct purchases and payments using bitcoins, thereby generating transactions within the system. • Individuals utilizing the Bitcoin system engage in the acquisition and payment for goods and services through the employment of bitcoins, consequently initiating transactions within the system.

• Miners: individuals possessing specialized skills and allocating computational resources towards the verification of new transactions and the creation of transaction blocks. The computations necessary entail a high level of computational complexity. As a result, these users are duly acknowledged and granted incentives.

Furthermore, apart from the aforementioned two categories, there exists a third cohort that is commonly neglected, namely developers. The principal mode of Bitcoin is its software, which entails the need for ongoing development and maintenance, thus necessitating the presence of a development team. There are six engineers responsible for the development of the current Bitcoin.org client, acknowledged as the "official" version. Nevertheless, due to the inherent nature of Bitcoin as an open-source protocol, individuals possess the freedom to develop various client designs, resulting in the availability of multiple options.

Notwithstanding their significance and particularly influential position, developers are incapable of imposing decisions upon the system. As an illustration, supposing the developers were to opt for an increase in the reward for uncovering a fresh block, elevating it from 50 to 100 bitcoins, it remains apparent that in the eventuality of dissent from the majority of users, specifically those commanding over 50% of computational capability, they possess the ability to transition to an alternate Bitcoin client that aligns with their perception of a justifiable reward. Under the most exceptional circumstances, individuals possess the capability to generate their own client, granted that it aligns with the established protocols. Therefore, although the developer's service is crucial, their impact is limited.

It is evident that the system engages the participation of both regular users and miners, with the latter shouldering the majority of the computational workload. It is crucial to underscore that government intervention is never deemed necessary. Should a miner choose to decline executing a transaction, it shall subsequently be conducted by an alternative miner. Due to the significant computational capacity demanded for transaction verification in contemporary times, the formation of mining pools has emerged, wherein cohesive groups collaborate to authenticate identical blocks of transactions and subsequently share the associated rewards.

As previously mentioned, in order to operate the Bitcoin network, it is necessary for the user to have successfully downloaded the entire blockchain and establish connections with nodes. This task is accomplished utilizing Bitcoin clients. Bitcoin clients are equipped with a functional implementation of the Bitcoin protocol. The Bitcoin-qt9 software serves as the designated client for Bitcoin transactions as per official standards. Bitcoin-qt downloads the complete blockchain dataset from its network peers and establishes connections with multiple other nodes effortlessly. Nevertheless, alternative methods of hosting a node have been developed. Alternative options such as web wallets serve as intermediaries that bridge the connection between the Bitcoin network and its users. When an intermediary is established, the users may not necessarily function as a node. This reduction diminishes the number of nodes and hence results in a decreased decentralization of Bitcoin.

In the forthcoming , we shall delve into the subjects of Instagram and YouTube, and explore various methods for generating income through these platforms. The rationale behind placing Instagram as the foremost platform within the is attributed to its widespread utilization as the prominent social media platform. However, the integration of these three platforms enables the potential to generate significant monetary gains. The majority of users generate income through affiliate marketing. However, in subsequent s, we will elucidate additional approaches for increasing your earnings by exploring diverse methods available for making a higher income. However, at present, we will elucidate the process of generating income through this approach and concurrently illustrate the integration of three additional methods that can significantly augment your earnings. Should you possess limited familiarity with affiliate marketing, I propose engaging in a discussion on the subject matter.

Affiliate Marketing

One could elucidate the concept of affiliate marketing effectively by employing an analogy. Suppose you hold the esteemed position of the university president, exerting a profound influence over every student in the institution. Given that you hold the esteemed position of president at this esteemed university, it follows that a significant portion of the university's population heeds your counsel and suggestions. Out of the blue, a professor from the university proposes that you take up the opportunity to sell their textbook. In exchange for your efforts in promoting the professor's textbook to your audience or followers, you would receive a commission or a percentage from each sale.

In summary, this could be considered as an instance of affiliate marketing. To achieve sales, it is imperative to establish a substantial following and subsequently promote a product to that particular audience. Simple enough, right? In this , we will delve into the strategies and techniques employed to achieve success in affiliate marketing. Now, there exist numerous techniques through which you can commence marketing a product to earn a commission. In this discussion, we will be examining the most optimal approaches for you to initiate affiliate marketing.

Presently, the techniques that will facilitate the commencement of generating income through affiliate marketing are YouTube, blogging, and the establishment of an Instagram/Facebook page. Now, these aforementioned three methods are considered the most optimal approaches when embarking upon the establishment of your affiliate marketing enterprise. Each of these tools presents advantages and disadvantages; it may be prudent to experiment with all three approaches in order to evaluate their suitability for your needs. Now, without any additional delay, we shall commence our proceedings with YouTube.

YouTube

YouTube was established on February 14th, 2005, by Chad Hurley, Steve Chen, and Jawed Karim, who were three former employees of PayPal. YouTube was initially developed by its founders with the intention of facilitating seamless video sharing, untouched by any associated difficulties. Advancing to November 2006, YouTube was acquired by Google for a substantial sum of USD 1.65 million. Since that time, YouTube has experienced continuous expansion. Based on various sources, it has been reported that on a daily basis, a minimum of one billion hours of video content is consumed by viewers on the YouTube platform. This serves as a testament to the immense size and reach of YouTube. Now, you may be pondering the possibility of leveraging the substantial popularity of this website to initiate the promotion of affiliate products, thereby generating lucrative commissions.

While there are certain techniques that can be employed for this purpose, it is worth noting that a significant number of instructional videos are being viewed on the platform of YouTube. At any given time of day, there are certain tasks that require your attention. Prior to initiating the promotion of your product on this website, it is necessary to conduct a thorough examination from your end. Rest assured, the task at hand is not arduous, resembling any business endeavor; its initiation will necessitate a certain duration and allocation of diligent exertion.

The initial step that must be taken is to establish a specialized area. Carefully contemplate your areas of interest. For instance, if you possess a keen interest in physical well-being, consider establishing a channel dedicated to fitness. Should there be an inclination towards science, it is recommended to establish a dedicated Science channel. One crucial factor to contemplate prior to commencing your own YouTube channel is ensuring that the subject matter aligns with your personal passions and genuine interests. This is the underlying factor that enables individuals to perceive the truth behind various matters in contemporary times. If one harbors a disdain for fitness and chooses to establish a fitness-oriented channel, it becomes apparent that their disinterest in matters pertaining to fitness is unmistakable, consequently dissuading potential subscribers from following their channel. Ensuring that you possess genuine affection and enthusiasm for the circuit you intend to build on YouTube is of paramount importance.

The second aspect that necessitates our concern pertains to the expansion of your channel or following. If an audience is lacking on your YouTube channel, there is a distinct possibility that your endeavors in affiliate marketing may not attain success. Prior to commencing the sale of affiliate products, it is essential to initially cultivate and expand your YouTube channel. Having acknowledged that, let us delve into the process of swiftly and effectively establishing your YouTube channel.

Presently, there exist numerous means to achieve the aforementioned objective; however, the most optimal approach that I would highly advocate for is the creation of distinct and original content. Although it may sound conventional, I assure you it is effective. Take a moment to contemplate. What reason would someone have to pursue your leadership if you do not present them with anything unique to benefit from? In considering the compatibility of your content, numerous approaches may be adopted. However, the primary approach to crafting unique material entails divergent thinking and forward-looking considerations, pondering upon what may potentially emerge as the 'next big thing.' Once such insights are attained, it is imperative to seize the initiative, ensuring that you are at the forefront of initiating the trend.

An alternative approach to increasing viewership and garnering followers would entail crafting captivating captions and employing clickbait techniques. Allow me to provide you with an illustration of a clickbait. In recent times, prominent content creators on the YouTube platform have resorted to employing attention-grabbing tactics, such as employing the phrase "My yearly income" coupled with an image displaying a substantial sum of money, as a means to entice viewers into clicking on their videos. As there is widespread curiosity regarding the earnings of prominent YouTubers, these individuals purposefully entice viewers in their videos, thereby augmenting their viewership statistics. However, they consistently refrain from disclosing their monetary gains. As previously mentioned, it is simply sensationalized content intended to attract attention. While this method does yield positive results, it is not universally applicable and may result in a decline in one's followers and other related outcomes. Therefore, exercise prudence when employing it.

.

Ultimately, the concluding strategy that I would wholeheartedly suggest entails engaging in fruitful collaborations with prominent YouTube creators endowed with substantial audiences. Prior to collaborating with prominent YouTube channels, it is advisable to ascertain the relevance of their content to your own channel. Forging a partnership with a major channel will prove to be a formidable and costly endeavor. Based on my estimation, the likelihood of individuals consenting to participate in a collaborative video with you and ultimately reaching a mutually beneficial agreement, be it through an initial payment or a shared partnership arrangement, is approximately 10%. There is a financial investment associated with this technique; however, the returns substantially outweigh the costs, making it the most effective approach to expand both your YouTube channel and business.

Now that you have successfully cultivated your YouTube channel to a significant extent, preferably with a following of 100k or more, the process of endorsing products for the purpose of earning affiliate commissions will be expedited. Once again, please bear in mind to endorse a product that is directly relevant to your YouTube channel. Do not anticipate successful sales of a PlayStation 4 through a fitness-related channel. It is not merely a matter of predicting that people will refrain from making a purchase; rather, it projects an undesirable image of you as a salesperson, which contravenes the desired impression you should strive to cultivate. Therefore, it is imperative to ensure that the product chosen for affiliate marketing aligns with the thematic focus and niche of your channel.

There exist several online platforms that offer the opportunity to initiate revenue generation through affiliate commissions. However, I strongly advocate for ClickBank and Amazon, which stand as the frontrunners in this domain. First, let us address ClickBank. ClickBank is an internet-based platform that offers a wide range of educational video courses spanning various niches, including health and wealth creation. Consequently, the website boasts an extensive selection of courses, catering to diverse interests and needs. It is possible to obtain a maximum of 75% of the commissions for every sale, which can be effortlessly achieved if you possess a substantial following. Your sole task entails appraising the video course and providing your audience with an authentic evaluation of the product. Please ensure that you include your affiliate link in the description section of the YouTube channel for the purpose of earning commissions.

Amazon is the subsequent option. It is widely acknowledged that currently Amazon holds the distinction of being the largest e-commerce platform globally. Furthermore, they offer a wide range of products, catering to diverse customer needs, thereby making it irrelevant which specific market you operate in. You have the ability to locate a product that is closely aligned with your specific niche. However, it should be noted that there are a number of advantages and disadvantages associated with this website. One drawback is that the commission rates are comparatively lower when compared to ClickBank. The precise percentage of commission is indeterminate, however the likelihood of finding a commission rate of 75% on Amazon is significantly more challenging when compared to ClickBank. Now, the advantage lies in the fact that upon a single click on your affiliate link, you will be entitled to receive a commission for all their purchases during the subsequent 48-hour period. This is the aspect where Amazon's lower commission rate compensates for its shortcomings. Once more, if you opt for Amazon as your affiliate partner, it is imperative that you thoroughly evaluate the product and provide a comprehensive review.

Ethereum And Investing

Similar to Bitcoin, investing can be done using the Ethereum platform. As previously indicated, both Bitcoin and Ethereum employ blockchain technology to store their transactions. Nevertheless, given that Ethereum is a relatively recent development, users may encounter certain disparities that differ from their familiarity with the Bitcoin platform.

There is a significant degree of speculation surrounding the potential for Ethereum to outpace Bitcoin, primarily due to the distinctive platform it provides to users and the continuous advancements being made by its developers and personnel to enhance the capabilities of Ethereum. Similar to Bitcoin, you have the option to invest through this platform and gain access to the various cryptocurrencies alongside the capability to trade them.

So, what sets Ethereum apart? As mentioned earlier, Ethereum is a decentralized platform that facilitates the autonomous operation of applications, effectively eliminating the possibility of downtime, fraud, interference by third parties, and censorship. In conclusion, this implies that in the realm of investment, Ethereum offers a greater degree of flexibility compared to alternative platforms such as Bitcoin, thereby eliminating potential limitations or constraints.

In order to engage in Ethereum investments, it is imperative to acquire a comprehensive understanding of its operational mechanisms. Ethereum operates through the utilization of contracts that facilitate the release of assets or values contingent upon the fulfillment of specified conditions. For instance, in the scenario where user A is required to access a designated website a prescribed number of occasions, said action must be performed in adherence to the stipulations outlined within the contractual agreement established by user B. Upon fulfilling the stipulated requirements, they will receive a remuneration of one Ether (a digital currency known as Ethereum) in consideration of their labor. This payment will be promptly dispatched and no further transaction is needed. Moreover, the blockchain system facilitates the transfer of program ownerships between users. Put simply, the contracts have the potential to be exchanged among users.

All transactions are conducted through an Autonomous Agent, which is a software program enabling the execution of transactions without human supervision. Similar to a cloud service, scalability is inherent in this offering, allowing for the seamless expansion of server capacity both in response to increased demand and to drive profitability.

Having acquired a basic understanding of Ethereum's functioning, it is appropriate to shift the focus towards its investment aspects. As previously indicated, Ether serves as the designated cryptocurrency for Ethereum, comparable to how bitcoins function as the cryptocurrency for Bitcoin. Ether is utilised for remunerating users upon the successful execution of contracts. In addition, Ether performs the crucial task of verifying transactions and ensuring their synchronization with the overall network, thereby guaranteeing an up-to-date and consistently unified state across all participants.

The distribution of Ether commenced in August 2015, through a crowdfunding campaign that spanned a duration of forty-two days. Approximately sixty million Ether tokens were allocated, while a total of approximately eighteen million dollars was raised to foster the ongoing enhancement of the Ethereum platform. This campaign ultimately emerged as the most extensive crowd funding initiative in recorded history.

When evaluating the investment prospects associated with Ethereum, it is imperative to possess the ability to scrutinize the intrinsic worth of Ether. In order to accomplish this, it is necessary to consider multiple facets including:

The increase in cryptocurrency trading within stock markets. There is a prevailing belief that the issuance and trading of stock on the blockchain platform will yield notable advancements as the future unfolds. The rationale for this is fairly straightforward. The present state of stock trading involves the involvement of numerous intermediaries to facilitate the execution of trades. Nonetheless, platforms like Ethereum eliminate the intermediary and facilitate the utilization of technology for stock trading. The exchange of stocks through peer to peer trading incurs minimal or no fees, consequently leading to improved profit margins for the stock traders. In addition to presenting a superior option for stock trading, there exists an entirely separate classification of tradable assets, including decentralized applications that encompass diverse components of various business models. Furthermore, this category comprises intellectual property rights and alternative tokens of value. In due course, blockchain will expand its application beyond the realm of shares, commodities, and currencies for commercial transactions.

Increasing ecosystem. During the development phase, the developers were concurrently engaged in compelling projects while preparing for the release of Ethereum. Some of the initiatives encompassed Augur, Weifund, and Colony.

Augur is a decentralized application (Dapp) that assists in forecasting market trends and predicting tradable options, while considering the network's influence rather than relying on a central authority.

Weifund is a decentralized application (Dapp) designed to streamline and enable the process of conducting crowdfunding campaigns. By means of Weifund, individuals possess the capability to oversee their own campaigns in addition to perusing ongoing campaigns, thereby enabling them to identify diverse investment prospects. Upon making an investment in crowdfund campaigns, you will subsequently acquire shares or tokens that can be traded on the reputable exchange known as EtherEx.

Colony: This decentralized application facilitates the establishment of decentralized organizations. Individuals hailing from various parts of the globe have the opportunity to engage in cooperative endeavors, in exchange for remuneration solely predicated on their contributions to the collective.

Comparative analysis of transaction volume and market capitalization. The price of Ether directly influences the quantity of transactions due to the incentivization of network nodes that rewards users for validating said transactions. Since the introduction of Ethereum, the volume of validated transactions has proliferated to approximately 15,000 per day. As Ethereum progresses and fosters the expansion of the aforementioned dApp ecosystem, a further surge in transaction numbers is anticipated.

The market capitalization of Ether is approximately one hundred and ninety million dollars. In the short term, it is highly probable that the platform's application demands can be adequately met by the existing supply of Ether. However, when considering the market capitalization, it is possible to perceive it as excessive, thus implying an eventual downturn. Nevertheless, in the case of cryptocurrencies, the speculation surrounding their future worth holds greater significance as a determinant of value, overshadowing the fundamental examination of the present utilization of a given platform.

Inflationary design. This factor ultimately determines the value of any subsequent distribution of Ether. When Buterin initially commenced his work, an inflationary framework was implemented for Ether. Hence, if the need were to arise, the distribution of the new Ether would be carried out on the network. The rationale for this was that Ether was regarded as a tool that would enable seamless execution of any transactions conducted on the network. If the price of Ether were to excessively increase, it would adversely impact the efficiency of the platform.

In the eventuality of this occurrence, Ether would cease to function as an investment asset, consequently exerting an adverse impact on the overall future valuation of any Ethereum-based projects. Upon examination of the present strategy regarding forthcoming allocation, it becomes evident that there exists a lack of lucidity regarding the course of action to be taken. Nevertheless, there are indications suggesting that inflation is poised to remain relatively subdued, hovering around the two percent mark or potentially diminishing entirely. Despite the inherent uncertainty surrounding the future distribution of Ether, it is important to acknowledge the persistent potential risk which might ultimately be overshadowed by the value derived from numerous other contributing factors.

In the grand scheme of things, it is widely held opinion that Ethereum will emerge as the preeminent platform facilitating captivating investment prospects. Upon closer examination of the underlying principles, it becomes apparent that the market capitalization of three hundred and fifty million appears excessively inflated given the platform's present utilization.

Nevertheless, over the course of time, it will become evident that the Ethereum projects will garner sufficient momentum, thereby leading to a stabilization of the market cap as the demand for Ether increases. When considering an alternative perspective, one may observe that the Ethereum project is currently in its nascent phase and, in the event of setbacks, it has greater potential for growth. Considering the growing traction of blockchain technology, it is anticipated that Ethereum will emerge as a highly successful investment opportunity upon its full release.

It can be quite challenging to navigate through the multitude of upcoming changes. Ensure that you prioritize your investments to avoid inadvertent overspending beyond your intended limits. Investments inherently entail certain levels of risk; nevertheless, in the case of Ethereum, the potential benefits may outweigh the associated risks.

Presented here is a sequence of straightforward instructions that can be adhered to when engaging in investment activities involving Ethereum.

Initially, it is advisable to establish an Ethereum Wallet. Your wallet serves as the repository for all the payments you receive or transmit. Regrettably, upon closer examination of Ethereum, one will observe that it remains a comparatively novel concept which is still undergoing active development. Hence, an online wallet that is entirely user-friendly does not exist.

Nevertheless, users who employ Ethereum have discovered that opting to create an Ether wallet proves to be more convenient by utilizing an online wallet generator. This particular tool grants individuals the ability to possess a public and private key, thus enabling them to gain access to their wallet.

There exist software applications, such as MyEtherWallet, which facilitate the generation and issuance of a tangible copy of your cryptocurrency wallet for secure storage. It is a highly innovative concept to incorporate the downloading of JSON files in order to create redundant storage locations for your wallet, thereby ensuring convenient accessibility.

When initiating a new transaction, it is essential to securely insert your private key into the designated location on the website in order to gain proper access to it.

Naturally, you would express a desire for Ether, the cryptocurrency commonly exchanged on the Ethereum platform, akin to Bitcoin. The most straightforward approach to acquire Ether is either through purchasing it or engaging in mining activities.

If you intend to purchase Ether, it is advisable to utilize the services of Shapeshift.io. This website offers a seamless user experience and does not necessitate user registration. It will also facilitate seamless transitioning between approximately thirty-three distinct cryptocurrencies.

The most crucial aspect to consider is selecting bitcoin for the Deposit Box and Ether for the receiver box. At this juncture, you will be required to input your Ethereum-associated public address and subsequently give your consent to the terms prior to initiating the process.

Once you have completed these steps, the system will initiate a deposit process in order for you to proceed with sending your bitcoin. After the submission has been made, you will subsequently observe a gradual increase in the Ether balance within your wallet.

In order to engage in Ether mining, it is imperative to possess a graphics processing unit (GPU) installed within your laptop.

Nevertheless, a more convenient approach to mining would be to acquire a cloud mining contract. This agreement grants you permission to engage in Ether mining on the Ethereum platform.

14: Dispelling Misconceptions Surrounding Smart Contracts

Smart contracts are of relatively recent origin and remain a subject of conjecture to certain individuals. As a result of this, several misconceptions regarding smart contracts have been formulated. Within this , you will acquire knowledge regarding the nature of these myths, as well as the veritable reality behind them. This endeavor will enable you to gain a comprehensive comprehension of smart contracts.

Legally binding

Smart contracts will be automated for smaller procedures; typically, they will be linked to a contract that possesses legal validity. Nevertheless, no legislation will explicitly declare smart contracts as universally legally binding across the globe. Therefore, smart contracts will have the capacity to incorporate a provision that is analogous to a conventional agreement. For instance, consider the scenario where you wish to market a vehicle equipped with a readily accessible button to be triggered as a contingency measure in case of non-compliance with payment obligations. Upon depressing this button, the doors shall be secured, thereby rendering the owner incapable of gaining access until payment has been rendered. Therefore, it is advisable to draft a contractual agreement incorporating the aforementioned clause, ensuring that the prospective buyer is fully informed and any potential disagreements are minimized, as all pertinent information will be unambiguously expressed in written form. Moreover, it will eliminate any potential for negotiation.

Nevertheless, the existence of these issues does not signify a lack of potential for resolution. A digital signature that is linked to a smart contract shall be deemed as a mutually binding agreement. Consequently, the individual accountable for their respective portion of the agreement will possess a clear understanding of the obligations expected from them. Furthermore, there will be no necessity for judicial intervention.

Smart contracts and Ricardian contracts are both important components of legally enforceable agreements.

Smart contracts have the capability to complement and enhance the functionality of a Ricardian contract. Nevertheless, they do not align with the Ricardian delineation. Ricardian contracts are oral expressions of a legally binding agreement that will render both parties accountable to a predetermined set of terms and conditions. The streamlining of the Ricardian process will be facilitated through the utilization of smart contracts, upon establishing and delineating the parameters and variables involved. Typically, Ricardian contracts necessitate multiple signatures, whereas a smart contract demonstrates superiority by commencing tracking activities once the initial signature has been affixed.

Smart contracts possess cognitive abilities and are capable of logical reasoning.

Smart contracts will consist of binary codes that shall ascertain the present state of the contractual environment, determined by pre-established metrics. Ultimately, smart contracts can be regarded as a form of artificial intelligence that operates according to pre-established conditions.

Beneficial for the fiscal industry.

Smart contracts will prove highly advantageous within the realms of the financial industry. Nevertheless, they can be utilized in any given sector where their usage is required. Smart contracts will possess boundless potential in terms of their applicability. Indeed, they possess tremendous utility within the financial domain owing to their invaluable contribution in facilitating settlements and providing indispensable support in the realm of loans. Smart contracts will serve as the repository of information for the individual possessing the investment. Therefore, it will eliminate the necessity of generating duplicate hard copies of documentation, which run the risk of being misplaced.

Beneficial for commercial endeavors
Valuable for professional purposes
Practical for corporate operations
Conducive to entrepreneurial pursuits

As previously observed, smart contracts possess the capability to be utilized across all sectors. Smart contracts prove highly advantageous for businesses, particularly in facilitating transactions involving goods and services. In this manner, there shall be no necessity for engaging in negotiations concerning the price or any conditions pertaining to the sale. Similar to what you witnessed in the previous car example, all the specifications pertaining to the sale will be explicitly stated, leaving no room for the buyer to claim ignorance regarding any of the conditions.

External factors

The utilization of oracles is increasingly gaining popularity, however, it should not be inferred that a smart contract can readily incorporate pre-verified conditions as there may exist nuances of variation. Smart contracts will ultimately ascertain the occurrence of a binary event. The addition of disparate variables will result in varied outcomes from different nodes, thereby rendering the entire process invalid. This is an obligation that you will need to address, as each node will verify the received information through the oracles whenever it is queried for data. A ten-second interval will ensue between each node.

Applications of Ethereum:

Decentralized Applications

Decentralized Applications, also known as DApps, are software programs that adhere to an open-source model, devoid of a single governing individual or entity, and operate on a distributed Blockchain or network of interconnected computers. Decentralized applications lack a central server, as the users establish connectivity with one another via peer-to-peer networks.

With conventional applications, they are governed by a solitary entity and operate on a centralized server, rendering them susceptible to security breaches or service interruptions caused by server unavailability. A decentralized application lacks centralized control, with no individual server or entity overseeing its functioning. It traverses a network of computers while alterations are determined by the users.

There is no singular focal point susceptible to server crashes or hacking incidents. In the event that a computer within the network becomes disconnected, the operational status of the application remains unaffected due to the simultaneous execution of the application on numerous other computers within the network. In the event of a network breach, wherein a computer is compromised, it remains incapable of executing unauthorized modifications to the application, as the consensus of the network's majority is required for any alterations to be made.

Smart Contract

Smart contracts are contractual agreements that are programmatically encoded and executed on a Blockchain or decentralized ledger system. The contract is automatically validated, executed, and enforced in accordance with the specifications specified in the code. Smart contracts have the capability to execute and enforce themselves, either partially or completely.

Smart contracts possess the capability to facilitate the exchange of valuable assets, as elaborated in the section discussing potential applications of the Blockchain. Accordingly, a multitude of industries leveraging Blockchain technology will employ smart contracts.

When a smart contract is executed on the Blockchain, it functions autonomously. Provided that the stipulations of an agreement are fulfilled, remuneration or assets are reciprocally transferred in accordance with the provisions outlined in the contract. Similarly, should the stipulations outlined in the agreement fail to be fulfilled, remittances may be withheld contingent upon explicit inclusion within the intelligent contract.

Smart contracts operate according to their programmed instructions within a decentralized network of computers on the Blockchain, thereby mitigating potential risks associated with unauthorized modifications, fraudulent activities, server disruptions, or non-adherence to contractual terms. The contracts are self-executing, facilitating the exchange of value and payments among individuals, thereby obviating the necessity of legal professionals or judicial intervention to enforce their terms.

The entries within the Blockchain are assigned timestamps and are immutable in nature. This establishes an optimal framework for contractual agreements, as any modifications made to contracts are chronologically recorded, while the preceding iterations are persisted on the Blockchain.

Contracts have the capability to be stored, allowing for the generation of new versions while simultaneously maintaining previous copies, along with precise timestamps on all modifications and amendments. It not only provides a more comprehensive depiction of the processes that occurred, but also fosters enhanced integrity among all stakeholders regarding the transactions at hand, as the ledger remains immutable. The Blockchain network obviates the requirement for the involvement of intermediaries in contract management.

Other Cryptocurrencies:

Dogecoin/Dogechain

One cannot discuss Blockchain without acknowledging Dogechain, which serves as the designated Blockchain explorer for Dogecoin, a highly significant cryptocurrency. Dogechain is recognized as a peer-to-peer and open source currency, thereby implying that its utilization is accessible to all free of charge.

Frequently, Dogecoin is referred to as the Internet Currency. Ultimately, it derived its name from "Doge," the renowned Shiba-Inu depicted in numerous ubiquitous internet memes, as well as the well-known electronic game called 2048. The Dogecoin Wallet can be found online, allowing users to access it from either their computer or other mobile devices. Although originally denominated in US Dollars, at present, users have the option to convert these funds into alternative currencies to facilitate seamless transactions.

In order to utilize Dogechain, it is necessary to initially visit the official Dogecoin Website. At that point, you will be inquired about your preference for storing your Dogecoin wallet, which may include options such as storing it on your Desktop, Online, on your Phone, or alternatively, on a Paper Wallet.

Once you have made your choice, you'd then be asked to choose the Operating System (OS) of your computer— either Windows, OS X, or Android, and you would then be given instructions as to how to access the wallet.

Upon adhering to the aforementioned instructions provided earlier, you will subsequently be prompted to initiate the download procedure of the wallet. A hyperlink would be displayed on the screen, enabling you to effortlessly initiate the installation of the wallet onto your device via a simple click. Upon completion of the downloading and installation process, you may proceed to utilize your wallet. It is anticipated that a waiting period of approximately 1 to 5 minutes would be necessary for the synchronization process to occur on all your devices, at which point, the task would be completed.

Litecoin (LTC)

Litecoin, formulated by Charlie Lee, an alumnus of the Massachusetts Institute of Technology (MIT), materialized as one of the earlier cryptocurrencies subsequent to the inception of Bitcoin. Litecoin was created with the aspiration of being acknowledged as the "silver" counterpart to Bitcoin, often referred to as the "gold." The developers aimed to develop an enhanced iteration of the original cryptocurrency. Mining operations, akin to Bitcoin, yield Litecoin. A significant distinction between Bitcoin and Litecoin can be observed in their block generation times, with Litecoin taking approximately 2.5

minutes and Bitcoin requiring approximately ten minutes.

Bitcoin and Litecoin are characterized by distinct algorithms. Bitcoin utilizes an algorithm referred to as SHA-256, which is a hashing algorithm that incorporates calculations that can be expedited through a process known as parallel processing. This factor constitutes a major contributor to the notable surge in the level of complexity observed in Bitcoin.

Contrastingly, Litecoin employs an algorithm referred to as "scrypt." This algorithm leverages the SHA-256 algorithm as well, yet its computations vary in comparison to the SHA-256 algorithm utilized by Bitcoin. Scrypt necessitates substantial quantities of high-speed RAM, as well as more than just sheer processing capability.

Litecoin has the capability to authenticate transactions at a higher velocity compared to Bitcoin. This signifies that Litecoin has the ability to efficiently handle a substantial number of transactions without encountering any obstacles. The swift block time additionally mitigates the likelihood of double spending attacks occurring, which is a prominent apprehension among numerous users in the realm of cryptocurrencies.

Dash

In the year 2014, Evan Duffield conceived a digital currency that was initially referred to as XCoin. After undergoing several name modifications, the cryptocurrency eventually underwent rebranding and acquired the name "Dash" in March 2015. Evan Duffield's motivation behind the creation of Dash arose from his observations during his analysis of Bitcoin. He was astounded by the technological advancements, however, he came to the realization that Bitcoin lacked the requisite speed and privacy. Rather than attempting to persuade Bitcoin developers to enhance the platform's anonymity, he opted to undertake the development of his own cryptocurrency. In addition, Dash functions within a decentralized peer-to-peer infrastructure, wherein the transactions conducted on the network exhibit an exceedingly challenging level of traceability.

It has been purported that Dash holds the attribution of designing a cumulative quantity of eighteen million coins within its overall supply. Currently, the current circulating supply of the cryptocurrency stands at 7.4 million and is anticipated to reach a total of eighteen million over the course of several centuries. Dash transactions are conducted at a significantly accelerated pace as compared to Bitcoin. DASH is available for acquisition through a reputable exchange platform called Changelly. The current state of the platform is such that it facilitates transactions involving 55 different cryptocurrencies. All that is necessary are your Dash address and a sufficient amount of BTC or LTC (or any other approved digital currency) to facilitate the conversion into Dash.

In addition, Dash exhibits distinctive characteristics, including...

• Confidential sending - A functionality that enables the discreet transfer of your funds, minimizing the ability to discern any individual transactions.

• Rapid transaction processing – Dash transactions are executed with remarkable speed, typically within one second – although this comes with additional fees for the expedited processing of such transactions.

• Master nodes – Within the Dash network, there are specialized nodes referred to as Master nodes. These nodes are equipped with privileges that enable the execution of Private Send and Instant Send operations, alongside the ability to acquire substantial block rewards.

The Prospective Value Of Bitcoin And Alternative Cryptocurrencies

There exists a multitude of more than 1000 cryptocurrency coins currently in circulation. The Blockchain technology demands attention and must not be dismissed any longer. Bitcoin and the altcoins collectively possess a total value exceeding $750 billion.

Certain individuals will amass substantial fortune while others will experience financial downturn, contingent upon the inherent worth of the cryptocurrencies in their possession. The primary cause of the majority of coins' ultimate downfall can be attributed predominantly to fraudulent activities, particularly in cases where said coins lack inherent value and are established solely to exploit the naiveté of unsuspecting investors.

Investing in alternative cryptocurrencies has the potential to generate substantial wealth with minimal initial capital, enabling investors to amass vast fortunes. Had Laszlo Hanyecz chosen not to exchange his 10,000 bitcoin for pizzas in 2009, he would presently possess an exorbitant sum of wealth.

An additional advantage of cryptocurrencies is that the majority of them serve as digital representations of access keys to a Blockchain, which fulfills essential functions of greater significance than the mere existence of the coin. To clarify, the coin is primarily regarded as an auxiliary means for facilitating value transfer in the majority of contemporary Blockchains. This ensures the longevity of the coin and its continuous functionality.

The value of the cryptocurrency will witness a steady rise as its users persistently recognize the significance of the Blockchain technology and consequently continue to actively utilize the coin.

10. Governing Bodies and Cryptocurrencies: The Choice between Prohibition or Leadership

Governments are equally perplexed by the exponential adoption of Blockchain technology, just as cryptocurrency developers have been. It appears that individuals had a deep desire to acquire financial confidentiality and the authority to exercise discretionary control over their finances. Nevertheless, certain instances are exceptional. Governmental entities have expedited the implementation of regulations pertaining to the management of bitcoin and the disclosure of information for examination. Nevertheless, numerous instances can be observed wherein bitcoin, altcoins, and fiat currency have been able to coexist harmoniously.

10.1. Japan

When Coincheck made the official declaration on September 13, 2017, regarding its acquisition of a legitimate license to function as a virtual currency exchange in Japan, the cryptocurrency community felt a collective sense of reassurance. A prominent global economic powerhouse has recently shown its support for Blockchain technology, despite facing significant criticism from China and the United States in recent days, which generated substantial media attention.

On April 1, 2017, Japan formally acknowledged Bitcoin as a legitimate means of payment. The government undertook this action in order to safeguard the interests of Japanese individuals utilizing cryptocurrencies and to establish a regulatory structure for their usage.

10.2. The United States

The United States could be implementing cohesive strategies to prevent the concealment of funds within cryptocurrency assets, consequently unintentionally fostering a broader understanding and appreciation among users of the potential capabilities inherent in cryptocurrencies.

When the Internal Revenue Service requested Coinbase to disclose the crypto wallet information pertaining to unidentified users spanning from 2013 to 2015, a clear directive was issued. The government was becoming aware and discerning the enigmatic situation. In instances where a substantial proportion of a nation's economic activity is inclined to shift away from conventional markets towards the Blockchain, there arises the imperative for regulators to explore avenues for regulation.

While this may be disheartening for those who desired to prolong their anonymity in the realm of Blockchain and accumulate untaxed gains, it is crucial for cryptocurrencies to gain recognition from governmental bodies in order to facilitate their wider acceptance in the mainstream.

10.3. The Republic of Korea

South Korea is regarded as one of the global hotspots for substantial cryptocurrency engagement. It holds the fifth position globally. The Central Bank in that jurisdiction has made a significant declaration, acknowledging the coexistence of both cryptocurrencies and fiat currency. Additionally, the government is actively exploring measures to enforce regulations pertaining to cryptocurrencies.

Section 10.4 pertains to Austria.

The Austrian central bank is adopting a prudent stance when it comes to the integration of cryptocurrencies. The esteemed Governor, Mr. Ewald Nowotny, has transitioned his perspective from drawing parallels between cryptocurrencies and the historical 'Tulip Craze' in 16th Century Holland, to expressing that the country cannot outright prohibit them in the same manner as a printed banknote.

At present, individuals have the opportunity to convert Euros into bitcoins at every post office situated in Austria.

Section 10.5. Spain

Spain has taken the lead in Europe by affirming that bitcoin is effectively a form of currency and is not eligible for value-added tax (VAT) exemption. This declaration signals Spain's willingness to embrace cryptocurrencies as an accepted medium of exchange on a larger scale.

In recent times, prominent financial institutions such as Banc Sabadell, EVO Banc, Abanka, and Banco Popular in Spain have entered into a partnership with BTCPoint to provide access to more than 10,000 ATMs for the purpose of facilitating bitcoin to cash transactions.

Therefore, with no commission applied to transactions, BTCPoint has effectively positioned itself as a direct competitor to Bet2Me, an alternative exchange that imposes a 1% commission fee in the same market.

10.6. The People's Republic of China

In light of China's status as a burgeoning economic power, the country acknowledges the imperative of assuming a pioneering role in the advancement of Blockchain technology. However, it has currently deemed it essential to adopt measures to regulate the emergence of crowdfunding.

They have initiated this stringent measure by implementing a complete halt of all trading activity on their primary cryptocurrency exchanges. Upon BTCChina's announcement of their intention to cease all exchange operations effective September 30, 2017, the subsequent aftermath was characterized by a substantial depreciation in both bitcoin and other prominent currencies, manifesting itself just days after the aforementioned declaration.

Nevertheless, it has been noticed that the Chinese government is collaborating with NEO to establish the pioneering concept of a Smart government.

Myths and Misconceptions Surrounding Cryptocurrencies

Due to the abundance of perspectives on cryptocurrency disseminated across various platforms, the task of scrutinizing an extensive array of resources to distinguish verifiable information from unsubstantiated claims might prove to be rather daunting. Similar to any other trend that arises in society, cryptocurrency is accompanied by various myths and misconceptions that bear minimal veracity.

If you are seeking to commence your utilization of cryptocurrencies, it would be advantageous to familiarize yourself with these fallacies and erroneous perceptions, in order to avoid being readily unsettled when encountering them in written or spoken form. These fallacies can manifest in various articles or blog posts, thereby diminishing the enthusiasm of individuals interested in initiating their use of cryptocurrency.

Presented below are the prevailing fallacies and false beliefs that contribute to the perception of cryptocurrency in a less favorable light.

The cryptocurrency market has reached its end.

Although a significant number of individuals have already embraced cryptocurrency, a growing consensus suggests that the trend is waning, with a gradual decline in its adoption. The reality is that cryptocurrency, despite being a relatively recent phenomenon, is gradually gaining traction. There are numerous varieties of cryptocurrencies obtainable in the market, and as individuals start to pay heed, their interest is piqued and they embark on educating themselves, ultimately leading to their participation in the cryptocurrency market.

Consider this, at the time of the automobile's invention and introduction, individuals regarded it as a perilous apparatus with potential to cause fatalities, and were skeptical about its ability to match the efficiency of the horse-drawn carriage. However, when considering the present state, it is noteworthy that nearly 90% of American families and households possess a minimum of one automobile within their premises. They can be observed across various regions of the globe, and a growing number of iterations are being introduced with novel functionalities.

Similarly, cryptocurrency possesses the capability to revolutionize the entire trajectory of commercial activities, banking operations, and financial procedures. It has the potential to enhance the efficiency, speed, and security of currency transfers compared to the current system in place.

Undoubtedly, cryptocurrency has yet to make significant strides before it could effectively supplant our conventional banking systems. Currently, the concept remains relatively novel and a significant portion of the populace remains oblivious to its applications and advantages. However, this does not negate the potential for its continued presence and expansion, impacting a wider audience globally.

Cryptocurrency attracts individuals engaged in illicit activities and those of dubious character.

It is a comprehensible misapprehension; however, it is entirely unfounded. The assertion that the utilization of cryptocurrency for drug purchases and illegal transactions on the darknet is solely confined to criminals and malicious entities, despite its widespread belief, lacks factual substantiation.

The dissemination of these adverse assertions regarding cryptocurrency restricts individuals from recognizing its potential in facilitating the interconnectedness and digitalization of financial markets worldwide.

Indeed, it is an indisputable reality that cryptocurrency is utilized for illicit transactions, perpetrated by criminals and individuals of questionable integrity. However, it should be acknowledged that the vast majority of cryptocurrency users are law-abiding citizens. They are able to perceive the ease and advantages of utilizing cryptocurrency, and as a result, they persist in employing it for their monetary transactions.

Let us consider an alternative tangible example - specifically, the realm of the internet. When the internet surfaced in approximately 1991, it was widely believed that its primary purpose was to facilitate the activities of criminals and purveyors of explicit content. However, if you observe its current state. Due to its remarkable and advantageous nature, surpassing its drawbacks, this technology has seamlessly integrated into our daily lives, facilitating enhanced interpersonal communication.

The initial apprehension surrounding a certain transformation ultimately proved to be advantageous for society - and there is reason to believe that cryptocurrency could share a comparable prospect.

Cryptocurrency poses significant security risks.

In fact, through diligent research and adept utilization of cryptocurrency, it possesses the potential to emerge as a highly secure mode of currency.

Cryptocurrency transactions are highly straightforward and uncomplicated; however, it is crucial to bear in mind that once a payment is made, it is irrevocable. That is the degree of speed and efficiency at which the process operates. Transactions are executed and finalized expeditiously, necessitating utmost certainty prior to initiating monetary transfer.

The responsibility for the security of your cryptocurrency wallet ultimately rests in your hands. Similar to a physical wallet used for holding cash, a cryptocurrency wallet comprises a cryptographic key that facilitates transactions. It is of paramount importance to maintain the confidentiality and security of this key to prevent any potential compromise to your account. In a similar vein to how you would prioritize the security of your PIN or other banking credentials, it is equally paramount that you exercise the same level of caution with your private key/s.

There exist various cryptocurrency wallet services to consider. It is advisable to ascertain which ones are the most dependable prior to making a selection.

Cryptocurrency is Expensive

Another fallacy that lacks veracity. In addition to the fact that establishing an account with cryptocurrency incurs no costs, the nominal transaction fees are inconspicuous to the point where they may go unnoticed.

Cryptocurrency serves limited practical utility

This statement is greatly divergent from reality. Cryptocurrency can indeed serve the same purpose as fiat currency, but with the added advantage of unrestricted usability across geographical boundaries. Cryptocurrency can be utilized globally, eliminating the need for currency exchange when transacting in different countries.

Multiple varieties of cryptocurrency can be utilized for the purpose of conducting online transactions. Many businesses have recently begun incorporating cryptocurrency into their payment options, capitalizing on its novelty by offering promotional incentives and discounted rates.

The cryptocurrency market has garnered a reputation for its inherent volatility, presenting adept market participants with the prospect of capitalizing on market fluctuations and exploiting the tendencies of individuals who are prone to hasty divestment when confronted with market downturns.

It poses a grave risk of instability.

It is widely acknowledged that the cryptocurrency market exhibits volatility, however, the level of instability does not pose a substantial risk. There are occasions when the market experiences a decline, however, such downturns are transient. Subsequently, should the market observe another sudden surge, individuals who hastily sold their cryptocurrency out of panic would have already incurred a financial loss.

Over time, the cryptocurrency market has exhibited a steady, albeit gradual, increase, thereby demonstrating that its volatility poses no inherent threat.

Closure of Cryptocurrency Platforms is Possible

This is indeed a legitimate concern shared by individuals: in the event that the cryptocurrency platform they have registered with is discontinued, what would be the fate of their funds?

Indeed, the mechanism by which cryptocurrency operates differs significantly. Due to its utilization of a blockchain and its collaborative nature involving a global network of users, cryptocurrency remains impervious to an immediate cessation. In the event of certain users being disconnected, counterparts from different nations persist in generating and conducting cryptocurrency transactions.

Cryptocurrency lacks legitimacy.

There exists a multitude of variations of cryptocurrencies available within the market, with certain ones even being deliberated upon within the pages of this book. Indeed, among the vast multitude of cryptocurrencies, it is possible that a few may lack legitimacy. However, this necessitates exercising utmost caution in the process of discerning and electing the particular cryptocurrency that one intends to utilize.

Acquire knowledge about the various types of cryptocurrency prior to making an informed decision. Acquire comprehensive information, encompassing both positive and negative aspects, regarding the various types, in order to enhance the likelihood that the chosen option is indeed legitimate.

Only the affluent can partake in cryptocurrency investments.

As mentioned earlier, obtaining cryptocurrency only requires a computer or device with internet access and the necessary funds for purchase. One does not necessarily require immense wealth to enroll and commence utilization of said service. It is open to individuals who possess the willingness to seize this opportunity.

Hence, those aforementioned are a few of the prevalent fallacies surrounding cryptocurrencies that may dissuade one from utilizing them. In the event that you encounter additional instances of such claims, it would be advisable to ascertain their veracity prior to accepting them.

Bitcoin Wallet

A Bitcoin wallet is a software application designed for the storage of Bitcoins. From a technical standpoint, it should be noted that Bitcoin is not physically stored in a specific location. Rather, each Bitcoin address is associated with a private key, which is essentially a confidential number, and this private key is securely stored within the Bitcoin wallet of the individual who possesses the corresponding balance. Bitcoin wallets play a pivotal role in enabling the transmission and reception of Bitcoins, while simultaneously granting users full ownership of the corresponding Bitcoin balance. The Bitcoin wallet exists in various manifestations including desktop, mobile, web, and hardware, constituting the four primary categories of wallets.

A Bitcoin wallet is alternatively known as a digital wallet. The creation of such a wallet is an essential stride in the acquisition of Bitcoins. In similarity to the digital nature of Bitcoins, a Bitcoin wallet can be regarded as akin to a tangible wallet. Rather than directly storing Bitcoins, the storage mechanism entails safeguarding a plethora of pertinent data, such as the secure private key required to access Bitcoin addresses and execute transactions. The aforementioned wallet variants comprise desktop, mobile, web-based, and hardware-based categories.

Desktop wallets encompass software applications that can be installed on a personal computer, conveying comprehensive administrative authority to the user concerning the wallet. Desktop wallets allow users to generate a Bitcoin address, which can be utilized for both sending and receiving Bitcoins. Furthermore, they enable the user to securely retain a private key. Several notable desktop wallets include Bitcoin Core, MultiBit, Armory, Hive OS X, Electrum, and so forth.

Mobile wallets are advantageous compared to desktop wallets due to the latter's limited mobility and fixed position. After executing the application on your smartphone, the mobile wallet will be capable of performing equivalent operations as a desktop wallet, thereby facilitating direct mobile payments from any location. Therefore, a mobile wallet enables the convenient processing of payments at brick-and-mortar establishments through the utilization of "touch-to-pay" functionality, which employs NFC technology to scan a QR code. Bitcoin Wallet, Hive Android, and Mycelium Bitcoin Wallet are among the various mobile wallets available.

Regarding web wallets, they afford you the convenience of utilizing Bitcoins across various browsers or mobile devices, irrespective of geographical location. One must exercise caution when choosing a web wallet, as it serves as an online repository for your private keys. Coinbase and Blockchain are widely recognized providers of web wallets.

The availability of hardware wallets is presently quite restricted. These devices possess the ability to electronically retain private keys and expedite payment transactions; however, they are currently in the developmental stage.

Ensuring the security of your Bitcoin wallet is of utmost importance. Certain measures that can be implemented comprise of securing the wallet through the utilization of a highly robust password encryption and opting for the cold storage alternative, wherein the wallet is stored offline.

How To Store

In contrast to conventional currencies, cryptocurrencies are characterized by their digital nature, necessitating a wholly distinct approach, notably in terms of storage. From a technical standpoint, the storage of cryptocurrency units does not occur; rather, safeguarding the private key required for transaction authentication is of paramount importance.

There exist numerous variations of cryptocurrency wallets to accommodate diverse requirements. If maintaining confidentiality is of utmost importance to you, it may be prudent to consider a paper-based or hardware-based wallet. The aforementioned methods represent the most robust options for safeguarding your cryptocurrency holdings. Additionally, there exist 'cold' wallets which are offline and stored on your hard drive, as well as online wallets that can be linked to exchanges or independent platforms.

How To Deploy Capital In Cryptocurrency: An Investor's Guide

If the concept of engaging in cryptocurrency trading resonates with you, we urge you to continue reading in order to uncover the steps and guidelines for commencing this venture. There are procedures to be followed in order to effectively engage in cryptocurrency trading. Allow us to carefully review each one individually.

Firstly, initiate the process by establishing a Trading Account

Prior to commencing cryptocurrency trading, individuals are required to purchase the desired digital assets. Purchasing cryptocurrencies is neither arduous nor intricate. They can be acquired through a cryptocurrency exchange or conventional brokerage platform. Some notable crypto exchanges in the industry encompass Coinbase, Binance, and Gemini. In the process of creating a crypto trading account on a cryptocurrency exchange, it is essential to establish a connection between your bank account and the exchange in order to facilitate swift fund transfers. Cryptocurrency exchanges impose a stipulated fee on transactions, thus it is necessary to conduct thorough research in order to select a reputable exchange that offers fair and competitive fee structures.

There is a scarcity of conventional brokers providing cryptocurrency accounts. Currently accessible choices consist of Robinhood Crypto, eToro, and TradeStation. Similar to its counterpart in the stock brokerage account category, Robinhood Crypto does not impose any additional charges for cryptocurrency trades.

Caution: Prior to making a decision on the location for initiating your cryptocurrency account, verify that they offer an extensive range of cryptocurrencies. Certain exchanges offer a wide array of approximately 50 distinct cryptocurrencies, while others provide a more limited selection ranging from four to five digital currencies. The greater the variety of cryptocurrencies offered by an exchange, the more advantageous it is for you.

Secondly, Select Your Trading Approach

There exist diverse methods for generating income within the realm of cryptocurrency. Select a course of action that is in accordance with your fiscal goals and capacity to withstand uncertainty. Selecting a trading strategy is of utmost importance as it will assist in the identification of cryptocurrencies that warrant investment in the subsequent phase. If one's schedule is limited, employing automated cryptocurrency trading proves to be an ideal trading strategy. It is possible that you perceive your trading abilities to be insufficiently developed. Under such circumstances, perhaps it would be worth considering the strategy of long-term holding (HODLing).

Third Step: Choose Cryptocurrencies for Investment

You may choose to commence with the widely recognized cryptocurrencies such as Bitcoin, Litecoin, Ripple XRP, Ethereum, IOTA, and NEO. Nevertheless, there is no requirement for you to exchange these coins as there are numerous alternative choices available. It only requires a significant amount of time dedicated to conducting thorough research on the investment options that align with your criteria.

For individuals engaged in day or scalp trading, it is imperative to select coins that possess substantial levels of liquidity and volatility. That would be an auspicious point of embarkation. Nevertheless, if you intend to pursue a strategy of long-term holding, it is advisable to conduct further investigation into the underlying projects affiliated with each cryptocurrency under contemplation. Choose a coin that you anticipate possesses a promising future. It is strongly advised that individuals at a novice level refrain from engaging in any trading or investment activities involving cryptocurrencies that have been recommended or selected by external parties. When financial losses occur, upon whom do you anticipate attributing responsibility? Is it not the person who made the selection for your behalf? Therefore, assume responsibility for your trading and investing decisions and carefully select the cryptocurrencies that you believe are most capable of meeting your objectives.

Observe their performance periodically after making your selection of cryptocurrencies for investment. It is impossible for any individual to operate a prosperous business devoid of consistent performance monitoring and analysis. You possess the qualities of an entrepreneur and it is expected of you to act accordingly.

INSIDER SUGGESTIONS

Please find below some recommendations to enhance your overall experience and increase the likelihood of achieving a successful investment.

Do not base your investments on emotional impulses - Practical investment decisions should not be driven by subjective feelings. If a coin exhibits significantly reduced value, one cannot make an investment in it solely based on subjective intuition. Conduct proper research, thoroughly analyze its past performance, trends, and base your decision on these findings.

Engage in Long-term Investment – This principle applies to all types of investment. Investing does not offer immediate wealth accumulation, as it requires a significant passage of time. When engaging in cryptocurrency investments, it is essential to anticipate a prolonged period of ownership. It is an endurance event, not a sprint.

Select platforms renowned for their credibility and reliability - When seeking a platform for your financial resources, the most reliable source of information lies in the experiences and opinions of existing users of the platform. Examine the evaluations and outcomes derived from diverse sources on specific platforms and elect the superior options. There is no greater disappointment than investing one's financial resources into something, only to discover the abysmal quality of the platform.

Exercise Caution Regarding Fees - It is imperative to exercise utmost prudence in this matter. Occasionally, there may be an initial proposition that appears to diminish the value of the coin, subsequently resulting in the imposition of substantial fees following the transaction. Prior to investing, it is imperative to gain comprehensive understanding of the undertaking involved.

Exercise caution against putting all of your investments into a single venture - This advice holds true across various investment strategies. When considering investment in your portfolio, it is advised to avoid allocating all your funds to a single venture and refrain from utilizing its entirety. In the event of adverse circumstances, it is imperative to ensure that sufficient financial resources are available to sustain oneself. However, it is advised not to allocate $195 of your bank balance towards Bitcoin if you currently possess $200.

Acquire knowledge – Although this advice may be apparent, it is often disregarded by individuals. When considering investment in the cryptocurrency market, it is imperative to ensure comprehensive knowledge regarding the coin under consideration. Stay abreast of current trends and devise strategies to track market developments.

Alternative Cryptocurrencies Suitable For Investment Besides Bitcoin

Investing in digital currencies is an increasingly competitive endeavor that favors those who swiftly embrace new technologies. Bitcoin has emerged as a pioneer, introducing the concept of cryptocurrency based on a decentralized peer-to-peer network. Furthermore, it has acquired the status of an established norm within the realm of digital currencies. Alternate currencies that draw inspiration from Bitcoin are collectively referred to as Altcoins and have made concerted efforts to position themselves as enhanced or adapted iterations of Bitcoin. Despite the relative simplicity and ease of investment in these currencies in comparison to Bitcoin, there exist certain tradeoffs such as heightened risk stemming from lower levels of retention, value, and acceptance. This book will primarily center on six key altcoins, carefully chosen from a pool of over 700, albeit without any particular arrangement.

Ethereum (ETH)

Its inception occurred in the year 2015, and it serves as a decentralized software platform capable of facilitating the development and execution of Distributed Applications (ÐApps) and Smart Contracts, all while ensuring an absence of external interference, fraudulent activities, service disruptions, or third-party control. In the year 2014, Ethereum initiated a pre-sale for ether, which garnered a highly favorable and substantial reception. Ethereum relies on Ether, a platform-specific cryptographic token, as the medium through which its applications operate. Consequently, it can be asserted that ether functions as a mode of transportation within the Ethereum platform, prompting numerous developers desiring to operate and cultivate applications within Ethereum to seek it out. In actuality, as per Ethereum, it possesses the capability to decentralize, encode, exchange, and fortify a wide range of assets. In light of the incident that occurred in 2006 involving the DAO, Ethereum experienced a division resulting in the creation of Ethereum Classic (ETC) and Ethereum (ETH). Ethereum (ETH) has a market capitalization of $4.4 billion, placing it second only to Bitcoin in terms of market value among various cryptocurrencies.

One recent significant initiative in the Ethereum (ETH) ecosystem involves the collaboration between Microsoft and ConsenSys, which enables the provision of EBaaS (Ethereum Blockchain as a Service) on Microsoft Azure. This offering empowers enterprise developers and clients to effortlessly access a cloud-based blockchain developer environment with a single click. In 2017, ETH undertook a significant initiative by establishing the

Enterprise Ethereum Alliance, with the primary objective of promoting and developing optimal standards and protocols to efficiently facilitate the integration of Ethereum technology within enterprise settings. Enterprise Ethereum consists of esteemed brands originating from the insurance, consultancy, technology, and banking industries.

Litecoin (LTC)

Inaugurated in 2011, Litecoin emerged as one of the pioneer cryptocurrencies subsequent to Bitcoin, often recognized as the "silver" complement to Bitcoin's "gold." This digital currency was devised by Charlie Lee, a notable individual with a professional background in engineering at Google and a prestigious education from the Massachusetts Institute of Technology. Litecoin primarily relies on a decentralized open source global payment network that operates independently from any governing entity. It employs a proof of work mechanism known as "scrypt," which can be efficiently processed using standard consumer CPUs. Hence, rendering it a highly decentralized open source. It is evident that Litecoin was designed with the aim of rectifying the deficiencies of Bitcoin, and throughout its existence, it has gained the endorsement of the blockchain industry, accompanied by substantial liquidity and trading activity. It possesses a higher rate of block generation, thus providing expedited confirmation of transactions. In addition to developers, there is a significant increase in the number of merchants that have adopted its use.

Litecoin has been designed with the intention of generating a larger quantity of coins, approximately four times greater than Bitcoin, and at a notably accelerated pace, equivalent to roughly a quarter of Bitcoin's rate. In general, Litecoin has been regarded as the second most valuable cryptocurrency after Bitcoin, although Litecoins offer greater ease of transactions and accessibility.

Zcash (ZEC)

Zcash is a cryptocurrency that operates on an open-source and decentralized framework. Its launch in the later months of 2016 has generated substantial optimism regarding its future prospects. For instance, if we consider the analogous relationship between HTTP in Bitcoin and money, we can draw a parallel with Zcash and its implementation of HTTPS. This alignment is in accordance with the distinctive self-definition of Zcash. It provides a mechanism for transactions to be conducted with a careful balance of transparency and privacy. Similar to the protocol employed by https, Zcash asserts its ability to enhance privacy and security through the inclusion of every transaction on the blockchain, while concurrently safeguarding sensitive information such as the transaction amount, recipient, and sender. The Zcash platform provides its users with the option of conducting "shielded transactions," which employ sophisticated cryptographic techniques to encrypt all data. Additionally, Zcash utilizes zk-SNARKs, a form of zero-knowledge proof construction, developed by the Zcash team, to further enhance privacy and anonymity.

To put it differently, Zcash can be regarded as an emerging digital currency and blockchain technology, which facilitates confidential transactions and the protection of sensitive data within a publicly accessible blockchain. It grants new applications, consumers, and enterprises the ability to determine the audience for their transaction information, even in the context of a global, unrestricted blockchain.

Monero (XMR)

It is widely acknowledged that this currency is highly elusive, confidential, and impervious to breaches. Monero is a decentralized digital currency, operating on open-source principles, establishing its inception in 2014. Its emergence has garnered considerable attention and intrigue within the cryptography domain and wider community. The advancement of the Monero cryptocurrency relies entirely on community involvement and generous contributions. This digital currency was introduced with a pronounced focus on scalability and decentralization, enabling absolute confidentiality via the adoption of a distinct cryptographic method called "ring signatures". The utilization of this technique manifests as a collection of cryptographic signatures, wherein at least one genuine participant is included, rendering it impossible to single out the authentic one as all of them appear valid.

Individuals who engage in Monero transactions have the option to convert it into US dollars or Bitcoin using various online cryptocurrency exchanges. Widespread adoption of Monero may be hindered if its utilization is perceived as potentially illicit or associated with dubious activities.

Ripple (XRP)

This represents a global settlement network in real-time, providing cost-effective, guaranteed, and immediate international payment solutions. Ripple (XRP) facilitates the expeditious and instantaneous settlement of cross-border payments for commercial banks, while also offering the benefits of lower expenses and complete visibility throughout the process. Introduced in 2012, Ripple currency presently boasts a market capitalization of $1.26 billion. The agreement-based ledger employed by Ripple, known as its validation mechanism, eliminates the necessity for mining, thereby mitigating network latency and minimizing reliance on computational resources. Ripple's core belief revolves around the notion that "utilizing distribution value as a potent tool can effectively motivate desired behaviors." Therefore, the present strategy entails the intention to allocate XRP primarily via enterprise development agreements, incentives for liquidity providers who propose narrower spreads for transactions, and the sale of XRP to institutional purchasers seeking to invest in the digital asset."

Dash

Distinguished by its former name Darkcoin, Dash represents a more discreet iteration of Bitcoin. It provides a higher level of anonymity due to its decentralized network architecture, thus rendering its transactions highly difficult to trace. Dash was introduced in January 2014, and swiftly garnered a growing base of enthusiasts within a short period. This cryptocurrency was brought into existence by Evan Duffield and can be acquired through the process of mining, which can be performed utilizing a GPU or CPU. In approximately March 2015, Dash underwent a rebranding from its previous name, Darkcoin. Darkcoin, an abbreviation of Digital Cash, operated under the ticker symbol DASH. Despite undergoing rebranding, they opted not to alter any of their technological functionalities such as InstantX, Darksend, and so forth.

Supply And Demand

Demand is contingent upon the prevailing price. In the event that the price of your preferred cup of coffee considerably decreases from $50 to $5 per cup, it is highly likely that you would indulge in a significantly larger quantity of coffee than your usual consumption, owing to the discounted cost. It's basically a steal. If the price of that identical cup of coffee were to inexplicably rise to $500 per cup, it is likely that you would find solace in mediocre instant coffee, as it would fulfill its purpose without causing any financial strain.

The central idea is that when prices decline significantly, it will lead to an increase in demand, thereby resulting in a greater number of buyers at that particular price range. Suppliers typically increase production of their goods in response to price rises, as this leads to enhanced profitability. Once the prices commence to decline, producers lack any motivation to produce beyond the essential amount as it would not result in any profits. Indeed, failing to reduce production could potentially result in financial losses for the company.

Price discovery is the procedural mechanism by which price adjusts in accordance with the forces of supply and demand. It serves as the convergence point for both parties, with the price point being highly flexible due to its reliance on the constantly evolving market conditions.

Through the use of various technical analysis tools such as straight lines and rectangles, trades have the ability to delineate areas of demand (support) and supply (resistance), thereby providing insights regarding the anticipated price range within which an asset is likely to fluctuate. Traders posit that the demand zone represents the optimal price point for acquiring the asset, prompting a subsequent upward movement in the market price. When the price reaches the resistance zone, traders perceive it as an ideal opportunity to engage in selling activities and subsequently generate profits.

Traders refrain from solely relying on lines to establish support and resistance levels due to the fact that these boundaries are better characterized as broad regions rather than precise points. To put it differently, the market does not consistently reach a definitive price level at which it reverses. It can be understood as a spectrum of prices.

The Bandwagon Effect

Technical analysis involves identifying the collective behavior of market participants and subsequently capitalizing on the resulting momentum by strategically positioning oneself in alignment with the prevailing sentiment towards buying or selling a particular asset.

Suppose there has been a newly issued press release. The traders deduced that the information was favorable for the specific asset or security under consideration, prompting an influx of buyers who subsequently drove the prices higher. Subsequently, you can capitalize on this upward trend and generate profits alongside the general populace. In cases of mania, traders exhibit a propensity to adopt bullish positions on a security without earnestly considering its underlying intrinsic value. They fail to evaluate the potential for profitable asset disposal. Subsequently, they find themselves in a predicament as they become the ones bearing the consequences when the bubble inevitably collapses. For example, individuals acquired substantial amounts of Bitcoin during both of its renowned peak points, without recognizing the fundamental principle that what ascends inevitably descends. Subsequently, there is a state of heightened anxiety, contrasting the phenomenon observed during a manic episode. Currently, everyone lacks rationality. They are eager to finalize the sales process without any delay. They fail to consider the necessary course of action. They exhibit indifference towards the substantial decline in prices and prioritize the recovery of their funds. At this juncture, their enthusiasm to enter the markets has waned.

These two circumstances are infrequently encountered in the financial markets, nevertheless it is prudent to acquaint oneself with them in order to adequately strategize. What factors contribute to the manifestation of irrational behavior within the market? Occasionally, the price may experience sharp, unforeseen surges or plunges within a span of one to two trading days. It has the potential to surpass levels of resistance or support, exhibiting characteristics of a 'breakout trade' that sustains the prevailing trend. Subsequently, subsequent to this period, the price may regress (or escalate) to the initial area of support or resistance.

Some trading perspectives suggest that it is advisable to wait until there is a slight breach of the resistance or support level and subsequently consider capitalizing on that reversal. One could alternatively opt to monitor the midpoint of the trading range, commonly referred to as the mean, average, or equilibrium.

Reversion to the mean is a statistical phenomenon that posits the transitory nature of both extremes, thereby stipulating the eventual return of a price to its average value. In order to engage in trading with this perspective in mind, it is imperative to carefully analyze the fluctuations in supply and demand areas, and subsequently execute trades in the contrary direction to their respective breaks. Others seek to engage in trade from the average to the outer margins.

State that the security exhibits a typical daily trading range of $10. It can be observed that the price displays a daily fluctuation of approximately $10, while maintaining a consistent average value of around $40. This indicates that if the present price stands at $35, it is equivalent to half of the established trading range beyond the average, thereby presenting a favorable occasion to initiate a short position. Price deviations should consistently revert to the mean.

The concept of mean reversion embodies the practical approach to trading. It is imperative to search for the mean price over a specified duration, calculate the disparity between the upper and lower prices, and subsequently initiate a long position when the price has diverged towards the lower or discounted section of the range. This method of trading is quite elegant when the market is experiencing consolidation, and there is an absence of a definitive bias indicated on the chart with regards to the prevailing sentiment of the bulls or bears. This can be utilized in a market that is currently experiencing a prevailing trend. The sole distinction lies in the necessity to periodically modify the aforementioned average.

Effortless Methods Of Generating Passive Income Through Cryptocurrency

Employing a multitude of sources of passive income is a prudent approach to facilitating the attainment of your specific financial objectives. Consequently, numerous investors and individuals have identified means by which they can effectively enhance their income streams in a passive manner. This could encompass a wide range of activities, ranging from the creation and dissemination of an e-learning curriculum, to the operation and management of an e-commerce venture utilizing a dropshipping model.

While a significant portion of the population is more familiar with generating passive income through traditional fiat currency, advancements in the field of cryptocurrency have expedited the progress of a novel digital economy that empowers individuals to create passive income via digital assets.

Engaging in the trading and investment of digital currency can potentially generate passive income for individuals; however, it typically necessitates further research and acquisition of requisite expertise. Furthermore, due to the prevalence of frequent fluctuations in prices and the inherent instability of the market, it cannot be regarded as a reliable and guaranteed means of generating income. It is an inescapable fact that seasoned investors also encounter financial losses during periods of market decline.

Therefore, it would be advisable to explore alternative approaches to enhance the efficiency of your crypto assets and ensure a consistent earning potential, even during unfavorable market conditions.

In the subsequent discussion, we shall explore various approaches to generate passive income utilizing cryptocurrencies.

1. Secure Your Assets by Depositing Them in a Savings Account Offering a Favorable Interest Rate.

While engaging in cryptocurrency investments enables one to capitalize on price appreciation, depositing funds in interest-bearing accounts allows for a more substantial income to be earned from one's crypto assets. There are currently a multitude of platforms available that provide this service to investors, with the majority of them encompassing supplementary functionalities designed to optimize the efficacy of your cryptocurrency assets.

Hodlnaut, an exemplary portal in this regard, presents interest rates meticulously computed on a daily basis, reaching an impressive maximum of 12.73 percent. Moreover, the platform offers functionalities such as Preferred Interest Payout and Token Swap, which allow users to acquire earnings and receive funds in their chosen currency.

Moreover, it is highly likely that these platforms will provide compounded interest. Consequently, it implies that you will accrue interest on a principal amount that exceeds the initial deposit.

This approach represents a highly impactful methodology for yield generation, regardless of the prevailing fluctuations observed within the market. What\\\'s the best part? There is no necessity for you to actively engage in its management. After the successful deposition of your currency, you are prepared to commence.

2. Cloud Mining

An alternative method of generating cryptocurrency through passive means is by engaging in cloud mining. In contrast to mining, which necessitates specialized knowledge and physical infrastructure for mining operations, cloud mining does not require these elements.

If one is not acquainted with the terminology, presented herewith is a concise elucidation.

Cloud mining is a process whereby cryptocurrency is generated utilizing computational resources offered by a third-party entity, commonly referred to as a cloud mining operator. In order to achieve this, you would be required to make a monetary deposit with a cloud mining service provider, who will subsequently utilize the funds to invest in a tangible mining operation.

You shall be entitled to a portion of the cryptocurrency endorsed by them upon its generation of rewards. Moreover, there are alternative options of cloud miners available to choose from, such as BeMine and Shamining. Some enterprises even possess mining facilities that are operationalized with sustainable energy alternatives like wind and solar power.

This approach presents a considerably more streamlined and efficient alternative to conventional mining techniques. The process is straightforward and does not necessitate a high degree of technical expertise or a significant amount of time.

3. Engaging in Investment Opportunities in Dividend-Paying Currencies

Acquiring and retaining dividend-bearing tokens presents itself as a straightforward and low-effort method to generate passive income through the utilization of bitcoin. Nevertheless, it is imperative to bear in mind that not all digital currencies offer dividends, and it is essential to thoroughly undertake your investigation before making any investment.

Presently, the majority of these digital tokens that offer dividend payments are being issued by exchanges. NEO and Cosmos are two examples of cryptocurrencies that provide dividends. Furthermore, certain tokens have been observed to provide users with the advantage of reduced trading fees, and in certain scenarios, grant them a share in the platform's profits. KuCoin Token (KCS) and Bibox Tokens (BIX) serve as illustrations of tokens that provide shareholders with dividends comprising a maximum of 50% of the trading fees incurred on their respective platforms.

One benefit of dividends lies in their consistent and unwavering nature, guaranteeing a passive influx of additional income over time. To enhance your dividends, it is necessary to acquire supplementary tokens and retain possession of them.

If you are in pursuit of alternative methods to generate cryptocurrency through passive means, we have delineated three straightforward approaches to enhance your yield. Furthermore, these activities do not demand a significant time investment, yet offer the potential for increased earnings with minimal effort.

Newcomers embarking on their digital currency investment journey may find it highly advantageous to deposit their assets into an interest-bearing account. No prior knowledge is necessary, and your task will solely revolve around conducting research on the platform of your choice. Once this task is accomplished, you will be eligible to commence earning revenue from your assets.

Four: Home-based Bitcoin Mining

The process by which Bitcoin is created

Bitcoin is a digital form of currency that is generated through computational processes rather than being physically produced like traditional currencies. Instead, Bitcoins are generated through a procedure commonly referred to as mining. Financial investors are increasingly resorting to engaging in Bitcoin mining as a means of acquiring digital currency. It offers a multitude of advantages compared to conventional currencies. The surging amount of individuals utilizing Bitcoin has led to its valuation reaching the threshold of $4000 by July of 2017.

If one desires to leverage the widespread popularity and exponential appreciation of Bitcoin, it is prudent to contemplate adopting the role of a Bitcoin miner. One can initiate the process of Bitcoin mining from the comfort of their own residence by employing specialized computer systems. There exist a group of individuals who are currently generating a steady and dependable stream of earnings by engaging in the practice of mining Bitcoin from the comfort of their own residences. The process of Bitcoin mining is carefully structured and utilizes cutting-edge software technology to ensure that only a predetermined quantity of Bitcoins can be obtained.

Bitcoin needs miners

Bitcoin enthusiasts globally engage in routine practices of sending the cryptocurrency to various individuals, most commonly, their own kin and acquaintances. Furthermore, they utilize their Bitcoin in diverse establishments that have chosen to embrace its use. Certain funds are designated for the purpose of purchasing goods and services, while others are allocated for investment or transferred to different individuals for various reasons.

The primary duty of a miner is to produce fresh Bitcoins and validate the correctness of every transaction. After being verified, the transactions are subsequently documented on the blockchain.

Miners ascertain the verification and recording of all transactions on the blockchain, thus ensuring their accessibility to every participant within the network. Individuals who are connected to the Bitcoin network possess the ability to readily observe and access regularly updated transactions.

This serves to underscore the significance of Bitcoin miners. They make a significant contribution to the efficacy of the Bitcoin system by verifying all transactions and upholding the integrity of the network.

Bitcoin mining conducted by Genesis Mining

Genesis Mining is widely regarded as a premier online platform for mining newly minted Bitcoins. Bitcoin miners have a limited set of responsibilities, comprising only two tasks;

• They authenticate Bitcoin transactions.
• They validate Bitcoin transactions. • They confirm the legitimacy of Bitcoin transactions. • They endorse Bitcoin transactions. • They ensure the accuracy of Bitcoin transactions.
• They engage in the extraction of newly minted Bitcoins

Genesis mining is a company that specializes in the mining of cryptocurrencies. The organization has engaged proficient professionals to guarantee a seamless progression of the Bitcoin mining procedure. A significant proportion of the professionals employed by this organization specialize in computer programming and software engineering.

Which individuals are eligible to engage in Bitcoin mining?

Individuals who possess an inclination may elect to partake in Genesis Mining, thereby commencing the process of generating fresh Bitcoins and affirming Bitcoin transactions. If you possess the financial means and are inclined towards investment, it may be worthwhile for you to contemplate participation in the Genesis Mining program. This specific product, made available by Genesis Mining, is tailored to individuals who are unacquainted with Bitcoin and the realm of cryptocurrencies. It is equally appropriate for investors operating on a significant scale.

Genesis Mining is the pioneering and preeminent service in the global market for large-scale multi-algorithm Bitcoin mining. It functions on a cloud-based infrastructure, enabling inclusivity for participants irrespective of their geographical location. This presents a prospect of exceptional value for investors seeking an opportunity to engage in Bitcoin and altcoin mining. Altcoin encompasses all alternative cryptocurrencies that present competition to Bitcoin.

Genesis Mining provides a superb prospect for individuals desiring to capitalize on cryptocurrency mining. Engaging in mining can be a fruitful endeavor; however, it will necessitate adequate proficiency on your part. The process of Bitcoin mining can be more easily facilitated through online means. The procedure is alternatively referred to as cloud mining as it grants access through a cloud-based network. Additionally, you have the option to engage in mining activities, which will enable you to secure a 3% reduction in price by employing the designated code LPQ5Y. Please refer to the following link for additional details: https://www.genesis-mining.com/.

Does engaging in Bitcoin mining yield substantial profits?

Bitcoin mining has the potential to yield substantial profits, albeit exclusively for individuals who are prepared to make considerable investments. It involves procuring the appropriate equipment for the task and adhering to the prescribed protocols. One can employ a mining calculator to ascertain the potential profitability of engaging in the Bitcoin mining process. A few of the elements that ought to be taken into account when utilizing a mining calculator encompass the subsequent:

Expenditure associated with the equipment employed for Bitcoin mining
Cost of electricity
Any expenses related to the recruitment of professionals such as software developers

Terminology related to the process of Bitcoin mining

Hash rate: The expression "hash" refers to a mathematical problem that necessitates resolution by the computer employed by the miner. Hence, the hash rate denotes the pace at which the mathematical puzzle is effectively resolved. An increase in the number of miners participating in the Bitcoin network leads to a corresponding rise in the hash rate.

Bitcoins per block: Upon successful resolution of a hash, which refers to a computational puzzle, a predetermined amount of Bitcoins is generated and subsequently introduced into circulation. The initial quantity of generated Bitcoins was 50, but it has now decreased to 12.5. Consequently, a mere 12.5 Bitcoins are produced for every successfully solved hash.

Bitcoin difficulty: The protocol of the Bitcoin network was intricately structured to permit the controlled issuance of a predetermined quantity of Bitcoins at consistent intervals of 10 minutes. Hence, the simplicity or complexity of resolving mathematical transactions will be contingent upon the quantity of miners present within the network. Problematic circumstances arise in the resolution of mathematical puzzles, particularly when the hash rate is elevated. Solving the puzzle becomes more manageable with a reduction in the hash rate.

Pooling fees: Bitcoin miners frequently collaborate in collective efforts aimed at distributing the computational burden of solving complex mathematical algorithms. A collective of miners may also be designated as a consortium, as they amalgamate their intellectual capacities, resources, and similar attributes.

Therefore, a mining pool comprises a collective of miners collaborating to enhance the efficiency of Bitcoin mining. The participants of the pool collectively contribute funds to a central pool in order to cover the expenses and overheads associated with its operation and maintenance. The pool fee is the term used to denote the charge imposed on each miner.

Energy expenditure: The act of Bitcoin mining entails substantial consumption of power. It is imperative to ascertain the power consumed by the computers in use, as it has a direct impact on the overall profitability. Hence, it is imperative that each Bitcoin mining pool determine the energy expended in solving an individual mathematical problem in order to ascertain the rate of power consumption.

Rate of conversion uncertainty: Bitcoin mining poses a challenge due to the lack of knowledge regarding the precise conversion rate of newly mined Bitcoins to the US dollar. The profitability status of Bitcoin mining remains uncertain due to this factor. This matter warrants consideration should you intend to engage in Bitcoin mining and retain the acquired assets.

Bitcoin mining calculator

Should you come to a conclusion that you aspire to pursue Bitcoin mining, it is imperative that you possess a mining calculator. This is a robust software application that facilitates the assessment of the likelihood of success in your Bitcoin mining operations. The calculator accounts for all the various factors associated with Bitcoin mining.

The essential requirements for achieving successful Bitcoin mining

To initiate the process of Bitcoin mining, it is imperative to possess a Bitcoin wallet as the primary requirement. Each Bitcoin wallet is associated with a distinct address. A digital wallet, such as the Bitcoin wallet, functions as an encrypted virtual bank account that securely stores the earnings acquired through Bitcoin mining activities. Additionally, integral are the tools required for the process of mining. Possessing the appropriate apparatus and implements is imperative. Herein lies an examination of several of these apparatuses;

GPU/CPU for Bitcoin mining: During the nascent stages of Bitcoin mining, miners frequently employed CPUs to carry out the mining procedure. Conventional personal computers were adept at managing the mining procedure. Presently, it is imperative to utilize a highly potent GPU mining system that incorporates advanced GPU graphics cards.

Contemporary graphics processing units exhibit a nearly 100-fold increase in speed and computational capacity compared to the central processing units utilized in the past. The higher the computing capabilities and speed of a computer, the greater the likelihood of success for miners.

FPGA Bitcoin mining: Manufacturers of Bitcoin mining equipment now have the opportunity to acquire and tailor kits utilizing a FPGA, also known as a field-programmable gate array. Utilizing this gate array enables the procurement of computer chips in large quantities, subsequently allowing customization tailored to the specific objective of Bitcoin mining.

ASIC Bitcoin mining involves the utilization of application-specific integrated circuits, commonly referred to as ASICs. These cutting-edge Bitcoin processing machines are currently being utilised as the most advanced and effective options available. These computer chips have been developed with the goal of delivering optimal mining performance at exceptionally high velocities. Nonetheless, the ASICS chips were engineered with specific functionalities, while consuming minimal amounts of electricity. Furthermore, the production costs associated with them are exorbitant.

www.ingramcontent.com/pod-product-compliance
Lightning Source LLC
Chambersburg PA
CBHW071656210326
41597CB00017B/2223